100 CHRISTMAS
COLORING BOOK

100 PAGES | 4 BOOKS IN 1

An Adult Coloring Book Featuring 100 Holiday Scenes
with Beautiful Decorations, Cute Animals,
and Festive Winter Designs

an Imprint of **The Fruitful Mind Publishing LTD.**
www.coloringbookcafe.com

Have questions? Let us know.
support@coloringbookcafe.com

 facebook.com/coloringbookcafe

 @coloringbookcafe

This Book
Belongs To:

Happy

Holidays

All is Calm

All is Bright

It's the most wonderful
time of the year

COLOR CHART

COLORING BOOK
Cafe

Thank You
For Your Purchase

We at Coloring Book Cafe are commited to deliver the best coloring illustrations to our community and we thank you for your support.

Please visit our digital store at:
www.digitalbookcafe.com

Claim your **FREE DIGITAL BOOK** at:
www.freecoloringbooklet.com

Find us on **INSTAGRAM**:
instagram.com/coloringbookcafe

Find us on **FACEBOOK**:
facebook.com/coloringbookcafe

Find us on **AMAZON**:
Search for "Coloring Book Cafe" and find our complete paperback collection on our Amazon Stores in CANADA, USA, AUSTRALIA & The UK

Printed in Great Britain
by Amazon

14183527R00127